Shit I did today

Kay D Johnson

Johnson, Kay D
Shit I Did Today

ISBN 978-1-989194-04-1 (pkb)

GoMe! Publishing

Shit I did Today is a unique adult dairy where you can 'journal' about the shit in your day.

As you can see, the date is left open ... because some days you just won't give a shit and skip that day.

There are no lines to stay between. Write where ever you want, it's your damn book.

And if you're tired or don't feel like writing ...

you can draw a picture of the shit happened during your day.

Don't like what you wrote ... rip out the page and throw it away.

It's your shit ... your book ... do whatever hell you want in it.

So go ahead ...

Let the shit fly!

Date:
Shit I did today ...
Shit I learned today ...
Shit I wanna do tomorrow ...
Shit I that made me laugh my ass off today ...

Date:

Shit I did today ...

Shit I learned today ...

Shit I wanna do tomorrow ...

Shit I that made me laugh my ass off today ...

Date:

Shit I did today ...

Shit I learned today ...

Shit I wanna do tomorrow ...

Shit I that made me laugh my ass off today ...

Date:
Shit I did today ...
Shit I learned today ...
Shit I wanna do tomorrow ...
Shit I that made me laugh my ass off today ...

Date:

Shit I did today ...

Shit I learned today ...

Shit I wanna do tomorrow ...

Shit I that made me laugh my ass off today ...

Date:
Shit I did today ...
Shit I learned today ...
Shit I wanna do tomorrow ...
Shit I that made me laugh my ass off today ...

Date:

Shit I did today ...

Shit I learned today ...

Shit I wanna do tomorrow ...

Shit I that made me laugh my ass off today ...

Date:
Shit I did today ...
Shit I learned today ...
Shit I wanna do tomorrow ...
Shit I that made me laugh my ass off today ...

Date:

Shit I did today ...

Shit I learned today ...

Shit I wanna do tomorrow ...

Shit I that made me laugh my ass off today ...

Date:

Shit I did today ...

Shit I learned today ...

Shit I wanna do tomorrow ...

Shit I that made me laugh my ass off today ...

Date:
Shit I did today ...
Shit I learned today ...
Shit I wanna do tomorrow ...
Shit I that made me laugh my ass off today ...

Date:

Shit I did today ...

Shit I learned today ...

Shit I wanna do tomorrow ...

Shit I that made me laugh my ass off today ...

Date:
Shit I did today ...
Shit I learned today ...
Shit I wanna do tomorrow ...
Shit I that made me laugh my ass off today ...

Date:

Shit I did today ...

Shit I learned today ...

Shit I wanna do tomorrow ...

Shit I that made me laugh my ass off today ...

Date:

Shit I did today ...

Shit I learned today ...

Shit I wanna do tomorrow ...

Shit I that made me laugh my ass off today ...

Date:

Shit I did today ...

Shit I learned today ...

Shit I wanna do tomorrow ...

Shit I that made me laugh my ass off today ...

Date:

Shit I did today ...

Shit I learned today ...

Shit I wanna do tomorrow ...

Shit I that made me laugh my ass off today ...

Date:

Shit I did today ...

Shit I learned today ...

Shit I wanna do tomorrow ...

Shit I that made me laugh my ass off today ...

Date:

Shit I did today ...

Shit I learned today ...

Shit I wanna do tomorrow ...

Shit I that made me laugh my ass off today ...

Date:

Shit I did today ...

Shit I learned today ...

Shit I wanna do tomorrow ...

Shit I that made me laugh my ass off today ...

Date:

Shit I did today ...

Shit I learned today ...

Shit I wanna do tomorrow ...

Shit I that made me laugh my ass off today ...

Date:
Shit I did today ...
Shit I learned today ...
Shit I wanna do tomorrow ...
Shit I that made me laugh my ass off today ...

Date:

Shit I did today ...

Shit I learned today ...

Shit I wanna do tomorrow ...

Shit I that made me laugh my ass off today ...

Date:
Shit I did today ...
Shit I learned today ...
Shit I wanna do tomorrow ...
Shit I that made me laugh my ass off today ...

Date:

Shit I did today ...

Shit I learned today ...

Shit I wanna do tomorrow ...

Shit I that made me laugh my ass off today ...

Date:

Shit I did today ...

Shit I learned today ...

Shit I wanna do tomorrow ...

Shit I that made me laugh my ass off today ...

Date:

Shit I did today ...

Shit I learned today ...

Shit I wanna do tomorrow ...

Shit I that made me laugh my ass off today ...

Date:

Shit I did today ...

Shit I learned today ...

Shit I wanna do tomorrow ...

Shit I that made me laugh my ass off today ...

Date:
Shit I did today ...
Shit I learned today ...
Shit I wanna do tomorrow ...
Shit I that made me laugh my ass off today ...

Date:
Shit I did today ...
Shit I learned today ...
Shit I wanna do tomorrow ...
Shit I that made me laugh my ass off today ...

Date:

Shit I did today ...

Shit I learned today ...

Shit I wanna do tomorrow ...

Shit I that made me laugh my ass off today ...

Date:

Shit I did today ...

Shit I learned today ...

Shit I wanna do tomorrow ...

Shit I that made me laugh my ass off today ...

Date:

Shit I did today ...

Shit I learned today ...

Shit I wanna do tomorrow ...

Shit I that made me laugh my ass off today ...

Date:

Shit I did today ...

Shit I learned today ...

Shit I wanna do tomorrow ...

Shit I that made me laugh my ass off today ...

Date:

Shit I did today ...

Shit I learned today ...

Shit I wanna do tomorrow ...

Shit I that made me laugh my ass off today ...

Date:
Shit I did today ...
Shit I learned today ...
Shit I wanna do tomorrow ...
Shit I that made me laugh my ass off today ...

Date:

Shit I did today ...

Shit I learned today ...

Shit I wanna do tomorrow ...

Shit I that made me laugh my ass off today ...

Date:

Shit I did today ...

Shit I learned today ...

Shit I wanna do tomorrow ...

Shit I that made me laugh my ass off today ...

Date:
Shit I did today ...
Shit I learned today ...
Shit I wanna do tomorrow ...
Shit I that made me laugh my ass off today ...

Date:

Shit I did today ...

Shit I learned today ...

Shit I wanna do tomorrow ...

Shit I that made me laugh my ass off today ...

Date:

Shit I did today ...

Shit I learned today ...

Shit I wanna do tomorrow ...

Shit I that made me laugh my ass off today ...

Date:

Shit I did today ...

Shit I learned today ...

Shit I wanna do tomorrow ...

Shit I that made me laugh my ass off today ...

Date:

Shit I did today ...

Shit I learned today ...

Shit I wanna do tomorrow ...

Shit I that made me laugh my ass off today ...

Date:

Shit I did today ...

Shit I learned today ...

Shit I wanna do tomorrow ...

Shit I that made me laugh my ass off today ...

Date:
Shit I did today ...
Shit I learned today ...
Shit I wanna do tomorrow ...
Shit I that made me laugh my ass off today ...

Date:

Shit I did today ...

Shit I learned today ...

Shit I wanna do tomorrow ...

Shit I that made me laugh my ass off today ...

Date:

Shit I did today ...

Shit I learned today ...

Shit I wanna do tomorrow ...

Shit I that made me laugh my ass off today ...

Date:

Shit I did today ...

Shit I learned today ...

Shit I wanna do tomorrow ...

Shit I that made me laugh my ass off today ...

Date:

Shit I did today ...

Shit I learned today ...

Shit I wanna do tomorrow ...

Shit I that made me laugh my ass off today ...

Date:

Shit I did today ...

Shit I learned today ...

Shit I wanna do tomorrow ...

Shit I that made me laugh my ass off today ...

Date:

Shit I did today ...

Shit I learned today ...

Shit I wanna do tomorrow ...

Shit I that made me laugh my ass off today ...

Date:

Shit I did today ...

Shit I learned today ...

Shit I wanna do tomorrow ...

Shit I that made me laugh my ass off today ...

Date:

Shit I did today ...

Shit I learned today ...

Shit I wanna do tomorrow ...

Shit I that made me laugh my ass off today ...

Date:

Shit I did today ...

Shit I learned today ...

Shit I wanna do tomorrow ...

Shit I that made me laugh my ass off today ...

Date:

Shit I did today ...

Shit I learned today ...

Shit I wanna do tomorrow ...

Shit I that made me laugh my ass off today ...

Date:

Shit I did today ...

Shit I learned today ...

Shit I wanna do tomorrow ...

Shit I that made me laugh my ass off today ...

Date:

Shit I did today ...

Shit I learned today ...

Shit I wanna do tomorrow ...

Shit I that made me laugh my ass off today ...

Date:

Shit I did today ...

Shit I learned today ...

Shit I wanna do tomorrow ...

Shit I that made me laugh my ass off today ...

Date:

Shit I did today ...

Shit I learned today ...

Shit I wanna do tomorrow ...

Shit I that made me laugh my ass off today ...

Date:

Shit I did today ...

Shit I learned today ...

Shit I wanna do tomorrow ...

Shit I that made me laugh my ass off today ...

Date:

Shit I did today ...

Shit I learned today ...

Shit I wanna do tomorrow ...

Shit I that made me laugh my ass off today ...

Date:

Shit I did today ...

Shit I learned today ...

Shit I wanna do tomorrow ...

Shit I that made me laugh my ass off today ...

Date:

Shit I did today ...

Shit I learned today ...

Shit I wanna do tomorrow ...

Shit I that made me laugh my ass off today ...

Date:

Shit I did today ...

Shit I learned today ...

Shit I wanna do tomorrow ...

Shit I that made me laugh my ass off today ...

Date:

Shit I did today ...

Shit I learned today ...

Shit I wanna do tomorrow ...

Shit I that made me laugh my ass off today ...

Date:

Shit I did today ...

Shit I learned today ...

Shit I wanna do tomorrow ...

Shit I that made me laugh my ass off today ...

Date:

Shit I did today ...

Shit I learned today ...

Shit I wanna do tomorrow ...

Shit I that made me laugh my ass off today ...

Date:

Shit I did today ...

Shit I learned today ...

Shit I wanna do tomorrow ...

Shit I that made me laugh my ass off today ...

Date:

Shit I did today ...

Shit I learned today ...

Shit I wanna do tomorrow ...

Shit I that made me laugh my ass off today ...

Date:

Shit I did today ...

Shit I learned today ...

Shit I wanna do tomorrow ...

Shit I that made me laugh my ass off today ...

Date:

Shit I did today ...

Shit I learned today ...

Shit I wanna do tomorrow ...

Shit I that made me laugh my ass off today ...

Date:

Shit I did today ...

Shit I learned today ...

Shit I wanna do tomorrow ...

Shit I that made me laugh my ass off today ...

Date:

Shit I did today ...

Shit I learned today ...

Shit I wanna do tomorrow ...

Shit I that made me laugh my ass off today ...

Date:

Shit I did today ...

Shit I learned today ...

Shit I wanna do tomorrow ...

Shit I that made me laugh my ass off today ...

Date:

Shit I did today ...

Shit I learned today ...

Shit I wanna do tomorrow ...

Shit I that made me laugh my ass off today ...

Date:

Shit I did today ...

Shit I learned today ...

Shit I wanna do tomorrow ...

Shit I that made me laugh my ass off today ...

Date:

Shit I did today ...

Shit I learned today ...

Shit I wanna do tomorrow ...

Shit I that made me laugh my ass off today ...

Date:
Shit I did today ...
Shit I learned today ...
Shit I wanna do tomorrow ...
Shit I that made me laugh my ass off today ...

Date:

Shit I did today ...

Shit I learned today ...

Shit I wanna do tomorrow ...

Shit I that made me laugh my ass off today ...

Date:

Shit I did today ...

Shit I learned today ...

Shit I wanna do tomorrow ...

Shit I that made me laugh my ass off today ...

Date:

Shit I did today ...

Shit I learned today ...

Shit I wanna do tomorrow ...

Shit I that made me laugh my ass off today ...

Date:

Shit I did today ...

Shit I learned today ...

Shit I wanna do tomorrow ...

Shit I that made me laugh my ass off today ...

Date:

Shit I did today ...

Shit I learned today ...

Shit I wanna do tomorrow ...

Shit I that made me laugh my ass off today ...

Date:

Shit I did today ...

Shit I learned today ...

Shit I wanna do tomorrow ...

Shit I that made me laugh my ass off today ...

Date:

Shit I did today ...

Shit I learned today ...

Shit I wanna do tomorrow ...

Shit I that made me laugh my ass off today ...

Date:

Shit I did today ...

Shit I learned today ...

Shit I wanna do tomorrow ...

Shit I that made me laugh my ass off today ...

Date:

Shit I did today ...

Shit I learned today ...

Shit I wanna do tomorrow ...

Shit I that made me laugh my ass off today ...

Date:

Shit I did today ...

Shit I learned today ...

Shit I wanna do tomorrow ...

Shit I that made me laugh my ass off today ...

Date:

Shit I did today ...

Shit I learned today ...

Shit I wanna do tomorrow ...

Shit I that made me laugh my ass off today ...

Date:

Shit I did today ...

Shit I learned today ...

Shit I wanna do tomorrow ...

Shit I that made me laugh my ass off today ...

Date:

Shit I did today ...

Shit I learned today ...

Shit I wanna do tomorrow ...

Shit I that made me laugh my ass off today ...

Date:

Shit I did today …

Shit I learned today …

Shit I wanna do tomorrow …

Shit I that made me laugh my ass off today …

Date:
Shit I did today ...
Shit I learned today ...
Shit I wanna do tomorrow ...
Shit I that made me laugh my ass off today ...

Date:

Shit I did today ...

Shit I learned today ...

Shit I wanna do tomorrow ...

Shit I that made me laugh my ass off today ...

Date:

Shit I did today ...

Shit I learned today ...

Shit I wanna do tomorrow ...

Shit I that made me laugh my ass off today ...

Date:
Shit I did today ...
Shit I learned today ...
Shit I wanna do tomorrow ...
Shit I that made me laugh my ass off today ...

Date:

Shit I did today ...

Shit I learned today ...

Shit I wanna do tomorrow ...

Shit I that made me laugh my ass off today ...

Date:

Shit I did today ...

Shit I learned today ...

Shit I wanna do tomorrow ...

Shit I that made me laugh my ass off today ...

Date:

Shit I did today ...

Shit I learned today ...

Shit I wanna do tomorrow ...

Shit I that made me laugh my ass off today ...

Date:

Shit I did today ...

Shit I learned today ...

Shit I wanna do tomorrow ...

Shit I that made me laugh my ass off today ...

Date:

Shit I did today ...

Shit I learned today ...

Shit I wanna do tomorrow ...

Shit I that made me laugh my ass off today ...

Date:
Shit I did today ...
Shit I learned today ...
Shit I wanna do tomorrow ...
Shit I that made me laugh my ass off today ...

Date:

Shit I did today ...

Shit I learned today ...

Shit I wanna do tomorrow ...

Shit I that made me laugh my ass off today ...

Date:
Shit I did today ...
Shit I learned today ...
Shit I wanna do tomorrow ...
Shit I that made me laugh my ass off today ...

Date:

Shit I did today ...

Shit I learned today ...

Shit I wanna do tomorrow ...

Shit I that made me laugh my ass off today ...

Date:

Shit I did today ...

Shit I learned today ...

Shit I wanna do tomorrow ...

Shit I that made me laugh my ass off today ...

Date:

Shit I did today ...

Shit I learned today ...

Shit I wanna do tomorrow ...

Shit I that made me laugh my ass off today ...

Date:

Shit I did today ...

Shit I learned today ...

Shit I wanna do tomorrow ...

Shit I that made me laugh my ass off today ...

Date:

Shit I did today ...

Shit I learned today ...

Shit I wanna do tomorrow ...

Shit I that made me laugh my ass off today ...

Date:
Shit I did today ...
Shit I learned today ...
Shit I wanna do tomorrow ...
Shit I that made me laugh my ass off today ...

Date:

Shit I did today ...

Shit I learned today ...

Shit I wanna do tomorrow ...

Shit I that made me laugh my ass off today ...

Date:
Shit I did today ...
Shit I learned today ...
Shit I wanna do tomorrow ...
Shit I that made me laugh my ass off today ...

Date:

Shit I did today ...

Shit I learned today ...

Shit I wanna do tomorrow ...

Shit I that made me laugh my ass off today ...

Date:

Shit I did today ...

Shit I learned today ...

Shit I wanna do tomorrow ...

Shit I that made me laugh my ass off today ...

Date:

Shit I did today ...

Shit I learned today ...

Shit I wanna do tomorrow ...

Shit I that made me laugh my ass off today ...

Date:

Shit I did today ...

Shit I learned today ...

Shit I wanna do tomorrow ...

Shit I that made me laugh my ass off today ...

Date:

Shit I did today ...

Shit I learned today ...

Shit I wanna do tomorrow ...

Shit I that made me laugh my ass off today ...

Date:

Shit I did today ...

Shit I learned today ...

Shit I wanna do tomorrow ...

Shit I that made me laugh my ass off today ...

Date:

Shit I did today ...

Shit I learned today ...

Shit I wanna do tomorrow ...

Shit I that made me laugh my ass off today ...

Date:

Shit I did today …

Shit I learned today …

Shit I wanna do tomorrow …

Shit I that made me laugh my ass off today …

Date:

Shit I did today ...

Shit I learned today ...

Shit I wanna do tomorrow ...

Shit I that made me laugh my ass off today ...

Date:

Shit I did today ...

Shit I learned today ...

Shit I wanna do tomorrow ...

Shit I that made me laugh my ass off today ...

Date:

Shit I did today ...

Shit I learned today ...

Shit I wanna do tomorrow ...

Shit I that made me laugh my ass off today ...

Date:

Shit I did today ...

Shit I learned today ...

Shit I wanna do tomorrow ...

Shit I that made me laugh my ass off today ...

Date:

Shit I did today ...

Shit I learned today ...

Shit I wanna do tomorrow ...

Shit I that made me laugh my ass off today ...

www.ingramcontent.com/pod-product-compliance
Lightning Source LLC
Chambersburg PA
CBHW081632040426
42449CB00014B/3277